Alaska Fishing Adventure

By Jim Bernard

Aka "Slice"

Contents

About the Author

Jim Bernard crossed the infamous Columbia River Bar at the age of 16 as an ordinary seaman. He graduated from a maritime officer's facility as a deck officer at the age of 21. He served in the Merchant Marine during the Korean War. He and his wife, Cherie, operated a fishing charter business out of Hammond, Oregon at the mouth of the Columbia River.

Jim has served as a captain and fishing guide in Alaska for the past 21 years.

Off to Alaska

My adventures in Alaska began when I noticed a small ad in our local newspaper, *The Daily Astorian*. It read, as I recall, something like this: "Fishing guide for southeast Alaska lodge," and then listed a phone number. I called the number and was interviewed by Bill Hack, the owner and manager of Yes Bay Lodge. That was the beginning of my Alaska adventure.

My contract from Yes Bay arrived by mail several days later: start date June 10, 1994; end date September 1, 1994; salary $1200 plus tips. So early on a June morning, off I flew for the Alaska adventure. I think I was homesick before I left.

Location and Background

Yes Bay Lodge is situated approximately 50 miles north of Ketchikan, Alaska on the Cleveland Peninsula, the mainland of Alaska. The site where Yes Bay Lodge is located had originally been a cannery. On or about late 1957, a group of investors bought the location and built what was going to be a gambling house and brothel. But when Alaska became a state on January 3, 1959, their plans had to be abandoned. Sometime in 1957, the Hack Family acquired the property, which was already operating as a fishing lodge. Their ownership has continued to this day.

The lodge is currently managed by Ryan Martinez. His wife, Niki Hack Martinez, is the chief chef. They each do an excellent job. Ryan meets and greets all arriving guests and is there to bid them a good trip home. He has an uncanny ability to remember all the guest's names. Niki, a graduate of a renowned culinary school, does a fabulous job as chief chef creating five-star quality cuisine. One of the guest favorites is her dynamite halibut. Art Hack, her grandfather and original owner, used to say "The fishing may be slow, so the food better be good."

Kevin Hack, the father of Niki, is the owner of Yes Bay Lodge. His knowledge of the area and fishing is remarkable. The tales he tells of the area are mesmerizing. His local knowledge is only surpassed by his knowledge of aircraft engines and float planes. He is considered a top expert in the field of float aircraft. He is a very astute businessman and a caring husband and father to his charming family; a very interesting person to know.

Settling In

Arriving at Yes Bay, I can clearly remember walking into the crew room to the staring eyes of 11 guides and saying, "I'm Jim Bernard from Astoria, Oregon." I had promised my wife that I would give her a call when I arrived. I made the call; at this point, not sure what I had gotten myself into. On the phone, I kind of whispered, "I'm not sure I'm staying. Let's keep in touch." But after a good night's sleep and the friendliness of the crew, I settled in.

Two of the senior guides, Mark Schaffer and Wade, spent the next several days showing me how to tie up the fishing gear and taking me to many of the key fishing locations. In those days, there was no GPS, so locating key halibut locations had to be done visually. So I was taught this skill. Needless to say, when those markers were obscured by fog or clouds— forget it.

My first experience halibut fishing took place in the Bell Island area. The spot is called the "Honey Hole" and is situated off the meadows in 310 feet of water. At that time, we dropped three lines as "soakers," no jigging. In short order, we landed 70, 50 and 42 pound halibut. I was taught to do the following—harpoon the halibut, then bring it to the boat, shark hook it in the mouth, take a half hitch around the tail, cinch it up and bring it aboard. This subdues the halibut and prevents injury to crew and guests alike.

For salmon fishing, I was taught how to tie up a two-hook salmon rig. We would use number 5 hooks and a 25 pound test leader, and either a whole herring or a "cut-plug" herring for bait. The cut plug is made from slicing a whole herring on a bevel (at a slight angle) just below the head. As the cut plug is trolled, its action resembles an injured herring, which to the salmon, appears like easy prey.

Each boat is equipped with two down riggers, one on each side of the boat near the stern (see example). After letting out approximately 25 feet of line with bait, a snubber, which is like a clothespin, is attached to the down rigger line. A 10 pound weight on the end of the down rigger line is lowered, which carries the fishing line and bait to the desired depth. When the fish strikes, it releases the fishing line from the snubber and "fish on!" On some occasions, we would use a "flat line" by passing the down rigger, attaching a 4 or 6 ounce weight ahead of a 6 foot leader and the bait. It would be trolled from 25 to 50 feet behind the boat.

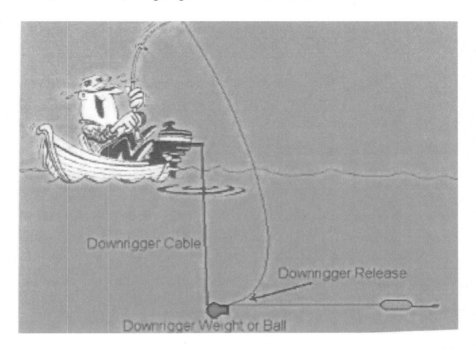

After several days' training, I was turned over to Bill Hack, who took me, or rather I took him, for my final exam before my first guest arrived. He suggested that we head across to Canoe Rock, which is about a 20-minute cruise from the lodge. Canoe Rock is on Revillagigedo Island, the same island as Ketchikan. They call the west side of this portion of the island the "face." From an aerial view, the north part looks like the "brow" of a person; the next prominent point the "nose" and final point the "chin." Hence, the face.

Reaching Canoe Rock, we dropped our lines and in short order, we had a fish on—but it acted funny. Instead of making a run, it went straight down. Bill fought it to the surface; it was not a salmon but a 30 pound halibut. In short time, we landed two kings. Bill was apparently pleased with my performance and gave me a passing grade.

First Guest

That afternoon, my first guests, a husband and wife, arrived. It was their first visit to Yes Bay. They came with a couple who had been to Yes Bay before. At that time, in June, we fished after dinner till 9 pm.

Bill Hack gave me the final instructions. He said to go to "Bluff Point," which is at the right entrance to Yes Bay, and then to troll hugging the wall. When I got to the location, the other couple and guide proceeded beyond us. We put out our lines and in short order, "Fish on!" The husband had a real hard-fighting king on. I had to maneuver the boat away from the wall. It made several runs—peeling the line out. I thought to myself—"Jim, you don't want to lose this one at the net." But cautiously, we safely led the big king into the net and into the boat. It ended up being just under 40 pounds. I was using my knife and accidentally made a big cut on my right index finger. I wrapped a small towel around my finger and proceeded to fish. Had another fighting king on; it was smaller, 17 pounds but chrome bright. A little before 9 pm, we pulled in our lines and headed into the lodge.

I felt extremely pleased with our success on my first trip with a guest. To the consternation of the other couple and guide, they never had even a nibble. (18 years later, the husband guest returned to Yes Bay and introduced himself to me. Sadly, he reported his wife had passed.)

When Bill Hack heard about my bad cut, he treated it and said, "We'll name you 'slice.'" Both the name and the scar remain to this day. In those early days, very few guests stayed out all day. Most came in for lunch. I guess a factor involved was the weather—it was much colder and wetter then. Every day was a long john day.

Surprising Catch

During my first year, I had a family as a guest, Mom, Dad, a 9-year-old son and a 7-year-old daughter. The dad wanted the children to catch rockfish. So I took them a short distance from the lodge to a rock slide area where we usually catch rockfish. The kids landed several rockfish, having lots of fun, laughing as each splashing fish came into the boat. I would put the lines out for them to avoid hanging up the on the rocks. We were in about 70 feet of water.

After landing several rockfish, as I was lowering the line, I felt something stronger than a small rockfish hit the line. I said, "Dad, you better bring this one in," and he said, "No, you handle it."

I set the hook and whatever it was dove for the bottom. I had to tighten the drag to gain ground. Little by little, I nursed the fish to the surface—as it surfaced; it thrashed and danced, throwing spray all over us. It was a 70 pound halibut. I successfully harpooned, shark hooked and bowed it with a half hitch and threw it into the well of the boat. Boy—what a surprise! But wait. A bigger surprise is to come.

Lowering the line a few minutes later, the same thing happened, but this time, the hit was much stronger and the fish was difficult to get off the bottom. Assisting the son, we'd get it partway up and it would dive for the bottom. Finally getting it to the surface—it was pretty well played out—there was no room in the hold of the boat so I lashed it to the stern of the boat and I towed it to the dock—it weight right at 100 pounds. What a rockfishing day! We were fishing in 70–90 feet of water where the rockfish are located. The halibut come up from much deeper water to feed on the rockfish.

Challenging Seas

I had taken two older Catholic gentlemen fishing at Bell Island, which is about a 30-minute run north of Yes Bay. We had landed several fish, including a nice king for each one of them. It was late afternoon, getting kind of dark. The wind was picking up, building white caps on the water. It was about 4 pm and our dock time is 5 pm. So I said "Ok, gentlemen, it's time to bring in your lines." Before crossing the Behm, I always switch to a full fuel tank to avoid tank changes in rough water. So off we go for the lodge. As we come around the north corner of Black Island into the Behm Canal, the wind had increased to over 30 knots (a knot is 1.15 statute miles per hour) and the seas had built to 5–6 feet. I made the decision to cross over to the west side of Behm Canal. Successfully crossing, I was attempting to follow the west bank up to the Yes Bay entrance. However, just idling, we were taking green water over the entire boat. Our boats are 20-foot glass ply with a canvas convertible top and 90 HP main engine and an 8 HP trolling motor, quite heavy and sea worthy. The sea built to 9–10 feet, and the wind just whistled. Finally a high sea smashed the boat with such fury it tore the windshield wiper off. With blinding rain, wind and seas, it was impossible to see. I had to hang my head over the side and then it was very difficult to see. Finally, after over 40 minutes, soaking wet and shaking, we made it into Yes Bay.

The two frightened wet Catholics went immediately to Bill Hack and said, "Bill—we were praying and doing our beads. But Mr. Bernard saved our lives." Many of our guides came from Florida where they fish in only 10–20 feet of water. So it's quite a transition to our deeper and rougher waters.

A Guide's Day

A typical day for a guide at Yes Bay begins at 5 am. Prepare bait and tackle, including preparing and baiting the crab and shrimp pots. Breakfast at 6 am. Take boat lunch to boat if on all day trip. Welcome guest aboard and record their license. Explain safety equipment and location. Launch the shrimp and crab pots. Spend the day fishing for salmon, halibut and rockfish, hopefully seeing wildlife, eagles, whales, porpoise and killer whales. About 4:15 pm, pulling our pots and rebaiting them. Return to the dock by 5 pm. Photos with guests and their catches; then processing the guest catch. All guides and dock personnel participate in this. Dinner at 6 pm. Then cleaning the boat and getting ready for the next day. Many days can be picture perfect—blue sunny sky, calm water and warm. Others can be like days made in hell—stormy winds, rough water, heavy rain and cold. We usually have one or two what we call "black flag" days—when the weather is so bad, we're restricted to the bay—or just the lodge.

A Day Off

When a guide has a day off, he often uses it to rest up, catch up on tackle update and repair. But often times, he takes one of the crew from the kitchen, laundry or bar fishing.

On one such day, myself and one of the other guides took the bartender fishing. She was an attractive small trim gal in her 20s. She had never been fishing before, but she wanted to catch a big halibut. We packed a boat lunch, thermos of coffee and a couple of bottles of Alaska Pale Ale and headed out in search of a big halibut. First we decided to try sea lion cove. We spent almost half an hour there without any action. I take that back— we landed a four-foot long shark with brilliant green eyes, which we promptly released. From there we headed to the Bell Island area and the "Honey Hole." We launched two lines in 310 feet of water and over the next two and a half hours, we landed five halibut, one flounder and several rockfish.

But the real treat was our bartender gal landing a real monster. It put up a great fight—several dives back to the bottom. She appeared to be getting totally exhausted, so we offered to spell her. She refused and finally got it to the surface—with a great deal of splashing and thrashing—covering all of us with sea water. We boated the huge halibut. It took two of us with great effort to drag it in over the side of the boat. All played out. She said, "I think I'd like one of those Alaska Pale Ales on ice." After we refreshed ourselves and enjoyed our picnic lunch, we headed back to the lodge with our catch. We were hoping the big halibut would exceed 100 pounds. Reaching the lodge, we weighed the big one first; it was a whopping 91 pounds—not over a 100, but what a fish. The next one was 55 pounds, the third 48 pounds, and then two smaller ones and the rockfish—a great day for a first time fisher person and what a treat for two guides on their day off.

Interesting Guests and Their Big Catches

I have a regular guest, Gene Alterman, who usually comes up twice a year in late June for the king season and in September for the silver season. He's a great fisherman. One season he kept landing a nice legal king salmon and I'd say, "Do you want to keep it?" He'd respond, "No—let's get a bigger one." This was repeated two more times. Then guess what? He didn't get another one that day. He ended up "kingless."

On another occasion, Gene had on a 30-plus pound fighting king. The king would make a run pulling off line. Gene was handling it like a pro—then all of a sudden Gene stopped reeling.

"Gene, reel!" or you'll lose the fish," I said.

"I need my Nitroglycerin."

After Gene popped a pill, we successfully landed a chrome fresh 30-plus pound king.

Another very special guest and friend is Pete Gwosdof. Peter and I have fished together at Yes Bay for over 20 years. Peter is very flamboyant, dresses like a classy fisherman, and carries some interesting gear. He has a duck whistle and call, which he blows frequently to spur the fish and fisherman on. He also carries a gold police-like badge. On one occasion when he'd been fishing for some time without landing a silver, he held the badge right at his fishing line and said, "I command you to strike." And guess what—bang! A big silver hit—true story.

We have several guests who love to test their skills by fishing with light tackle. One Hawaiian guest had claimed the world's title two years earlier by landing the largest silver on 2 pound test line. But he'd lost the year before and was here to attempt to regain the title. I had the "unfortunate" challenge of being his guide.

He'd get a nice silver on and I would carefully maneuver the boat so not too much stress was put on the line. Sometimes I would be going around in circles for up to 30 minutes—then the fish would make a sudden jerk and "snap," it would be gone. We did land several silver, but they didn't appear to be in a judging range. The record to win was 12.8 pounds or thereabouts. Finally we had what appeared to be a qualifier. It was on for over 55 minutes. I was so tired of circling and circling, I could have cut the line—but the fish did it for me. I think the guest, also tired, apparently put too much pressure on the line and it snapped, "Thank God!"

I spent three days doing the same thing. As the guest left, he thanked me and gave me a box of Hawaiian macadamia candy and $50 tip. "I'll ask for you next year. Thanks?"

One of our longtime guests, Gus Armstrong, also enjoys the challenge of fishing for salmon with light line. He is really a skilled fisherman and usually gets his fish. One time when we fished together, he hooked, as I recall, a 30 pound king at Bell Island. It really took off—in fact, he hooked it in the upper drift and almost an hour later, we finally landed it on the opposite side of the stream.

Earlier this season, in fact it was the 4th of July, fishing with a regular guest, a very experienced fisherman, Henry Liebman. We landed the largest king salmon of the season. We were fishing a white spoon at 60 feet. We were trolling at Bell Island near the big white rock down from the meadows in 200 feet of water near the shore. When the king hit, it took off like greased lightning. The line was just screaming and frantically I turned the boat around and had to chase the fish as the reel was almost spooled. Henry would recover a little line and off the king would go. Two other boats close by gave us courtesy and maneuvered their boats clear of our action. Finally after a truly king fight, we nursed the great king near the boat. I couldn't believe the size—will it fit in the net? It was not only fat and of great girth, but long, and I prayed, "Lord help me get it in the net." I lowered the net to the water and asked Henry to walk back as we gently led the chrome beauty into the net—we listed it on Henry's fishing license and fired up the big engine and headed back to the dock to weigh our catch. The record fish up to this point was 38.7 pounds. Back at the dock, we lifted our beauty onto the scales with "bated breath" and watching as the scale moved to 43.8 pounds. A big roar of applause came from the bystanders. That was one of the largest kings landed in my boat during my 21 years at Yes Bay. The largest halibut was a 156 pound landed with another guide in the "Honey Hole" off the meadows in 310 feet of water near Bell Island. It took 30 minutes to land.

Strange Things

Many strange and unusual things have happened while fishing in Alaska. One time while fishing on the drift at Bell Island close to other boats near shore, a large 30-plus pound king hit our line and took off between boats. It went toward the middle of the stream and back—jumped once and then sounded and disappeared—where did it go? I thought. Then I hear a splash-like sound and something hits me hard on the back and the fish glanced off my shoulder and landed on the deck of our boat. Nearby boats witnessed it and I quickly gave it a hardy hit to prevent it from jumping overboard.

Another odd one. We were fishing for halibut off Gedney Island in a now forgotten halibut spot. Bang! A big strike—Good! A halibut on. The guest struggled to get it to the surface. A halibut, no? But what is it? Low and behold, it was a huge 80-plus pound octopus—a huge head and long tentacles reaching every which way. The guest insisted that we release it, which we did.

Another surprise catch occurred fishing for salmon at Bell Island when, toward the end of the drift, "Fish on!" Felt like a real nice king, but when it surfaced near our boat—a king? No. What is it? It turned out to be a beautiful (if you call any lingcod beautiful) 21.3 pound lingcod—ok, we'll take it.

On another occasion, I had two gentlemen guests. One was 87 and had just learned how to ski, and the other was 91. Both were slim and in good shape. We were halibut fishing on what we refer to as the "main," situated at the east end of Spacious Bay—about a 20-minute run from the lodge. We were fishing in 310 feet of water. The guests were what we call soaking their bait but occasionally raising it off the bottom and up a couple of turns. It was a very sunny warm afternoon, and both guests had drifted off to slumberland, so I was working their lines. As I was lowering the older man's line, I felt a strange hit and then nothing. Seconds later, a big hit and the line took off. I woke the guests up and said, "I think you have a big king on." Boy did it take off. The guest struggled with it and finally said, "Mr. Bernard, I can't handle it. You take it." By this time, it was actually pulling our boat—I couldn't gain any line on it. After tightening the drag, it made a heavy jerk and the line parted.

When I reported the event to Bill Hack, he was certain that it was a salmon shark. They are 10–12 feet in length and can travel up to 50 miles an hour. The guest didn't get a halibut, but an exciting adventure.

Alaska's Wildlife

The wildlife in Alaska is awe-striking—humpback whales, porpoise, killer whales, sea lions, elephant seals and eagles. On one occasion a humpback whale breached right under one of our boats, frightening the heck out of the guide and guest.

Fishing near the meadow with two guests, a killer whale breached within 50 feet of our boat 6 feet off the water perfectly horizontal. What a sight. One of the guests got an excellent picture of it.

Many years ago when Bill Hack was a young kid, he accidentally ran over a young killer whale, cutting its vertical fin. Now each year, grown, the whale returns to the lodge, and with its bent fin; we call him "Ole' Bent Fin." He appears as if to haunt us.

A Bear Scare

During one of my early years at Yes Bay, I was picked to lead a group of five male guests to the Anan bear lookout. It's about a 20-minute flight from Yes Bay. The flight to Anan took us over partially snow-clad peaks. The pilot spotted mountain goats on one peak. He circled slowly so we got an excellent view of the white mountain goats.

Landing in the bay at Anan, we were met by a forest ranger. He pointed us to the trail to the lower bear lookout. I led the guests, instructing them that the most danger from bear is surprising them. So on each blind turn on the trail, we clapped our hands and said, "Here, bear; here, bear." The other danger is getting between a sow and her cubs.

Reaching the lower bear lookout, we were disappointed as there were no bear. I'd been informed by Bill Hack that after being closed for five years, the upper lookout was now open. Another forest ranger had met us at the lower lookout. I said that we'd like to go to the upper lookout. He said the reason it had been closed was that there had been several bear attacks up there, one fatal. Desiring to have our guest see bear, I said we'd like to proceed to the lookout. He advised us against it. But I persisted. So he insisted that I make the 20-minute hike with him first before taking the guests. So I took off with the ranger. A short distance from the upper lookout, we had a walkie-talkie call from a ranger at the upper lookout, in fact yelling, "Stop where you are! There's a large sow to the left of the trail and her two cubs are on the right of the trail." You're right in between them. Needless to say, I was a bit frightened. We could see both the sow and her cubs. After waiting for what seemed like an eternity, the sow crossed the trail above us and joined her cubs.

At the upper lookout, there were lots of bears to view. But I had to make the trek back to the lower lookout and retrieve my guests for the venture back to the upper lookout. By the time I reached the lower lookout, two of the guests had backed out. Without any further danger, we successfully reached the upper lookout and enjoyed seeing bear feasting on salmon. We took pictures and returned down the trail to meet our waiting plane.

Each day in Alaska is a new adventure. You never know what exciting event awaits you.

A Close Call

Big winds and storms can come up in our area without much warning. When one such storm came up, one of our boats was trapped with guests in "Convenience Cove," a protected area between Hassler and Gedney Islands at the east side of the Behm Canal. The winds were blowing at 40-plus knots and the seas had built from 5 to 10 feet. Finally the guide got tired of waiting and made a dangerous attempt to cross. He was hit and tossed and battered by the thrashing seas. In the middle of the Behm, the boat was pounded with such force, it knocked the top off the boat and broke the windshield out. Frightened and soaking wet, they finally made it across.

In my 21 years at Yes Bay, no one has lost their life from the sea.

Even other wildlife like to participate in salmon fishing. Several times, our boat would be surrounded by porpoise. They'd dive and splash all around our boat. Then all of a sudden, a singing of our line going out, a porpoise had taken off with our bait; immediately I cut the line.

On several occasions while bringing in an under-sized king, the sharp eye of an eagle would spot it and from its perch would dive down and grab the small salmon with his talons and away he'd fly. Fish still attached to our line, so we were actually flying the eagle like a kite—but soon it would come loose.

Another time we had a silver salmon on—as the guest brought it closer to the stern of the boat, all of a sudden I heard a loud growling sound and only two feet from me was a large sea lion—he'd just swallowed my 10 inch silver dodger and with the line still attached, the silver was flopping around his head as he swam off.

Near the lodge, an eagle had sunk his talons into the carcass of a large yellow eye red snapper, unable to get airborne. It used its wings as paddles and paddled to shore with its prey.

Crazy Crew (but Good)

It's interesting to wonder what brings members of our crew to Alaska. Are they (including me) running away from something or in search of themselves or adventure?

We had one guide, nice looking in his 30s, a big man, 6 feet and 250 pounds and oh, how he loved to drink. He even had a coat designed—for drinker's ice storage for cans of beer and a pocket for a flask. He was a good fisherman, but his drinking got him a trip home.

Then there was "Chubby," 5 feet 6 inches and 300 pounds. A great fisherman, but oh, how he could eat and cook. He made the best biscuits and gravy. He included for extra character a generous dose of Jack Daniels. His problem was that after eating, he'd get sleepy. Several times while trolling after lunch, he'd fall asleep at the helm and the guest would have to wake him up.

Then there was Richard, one of our guides. He was nicknamed "Magellan" as he kept getting lost with his guests. He'd call in—"I'm lost."

"What does it look like where you are?"

"Trees and rocks."

Big help.

And there was Drue—a very talented fisherman, but if he didn't like his guest, he wouldn't help them catch fish. All the other boats would come in with limits of fish and here would come Drue holding only one small dried out pink salmon.

And then there was "Slammer," tall and kind of lanky. Always wore white boots. He was very superstitious. If you wished him good luck, it was bad luck. He never uttered the word thirteen; it was always twelve plus one.

Bananas—never! "No bananas on my boat. Never whistle on my boat!" I guess a lot of that comes down from fisherman and sea merchants in the past—like never leave port on a Friday. I forget to mention, Slammer is an excellent fisherman.

Slammer and I were halibut fishing near the entrance to Yes Bay in 300 feet of water. In short time, we hooked into a very large halibut; when we got it to the surface, both of our hooks were in this mammoth fish. Slammer said, "Slice, you harpoon it." I took careful aim and slammed the spear into the halibut, but it didn't go all the way through and the monster dove 300-plus feet to the bottom. After what seemed like an eternity, we had it to the surface and successfully harpooned and boated what turned out to be 107 pound halibut.

I guess I'd better also mention "Kicker." Kicker is an excellent fisherman, short and stocky with dark complexion and dark hair; he kind of shuffles along because of foot problems. I tell you this; he's in total command of his boat and guest. He doesn't ask them to "sit down" or "reel," he commands them. He's the only guide I know who can totally insult a guest and get away with it—they learn to love him.

Another great guide and fisherman is "Batman," David Noble. A funny thing happened aboard David Noble's boat. A fish was playing with a guest's line and David had instructed the guest to be alert and hit or set the line when a fish struck. As the fish made a more aggressive move on the line, David yelled out, "Hit it, you son of a bitch!" The guest thought David was talking to him, so he set the line. David's comment was meant for the fish. After David apologized, they all had a good laugh. David, sometime later, received a silver dodger from the guest with these words inscribed on it, "Hit it, you son of a bitch. Thanks, David."

Also deserving mention are a husband and wife guiding team, Capt. Al and Capt. Tina—"Snapper" and "Ol' Spice." I've never known a woman who can fish the way Ol' Spice can—most of the time out fishing the male guides—and she tops it all off with a pleasing personality. Al is equally effective—a great fisherman—real nice guy and probably takes credit for training Tina.

The rest of this year's guides all deserve credit for their expert fishing ability. Jon, "Son of Zebedee," Guy, "Piano Man," Troy, "Eclipse," Chris, "Rapchick" and Andrew, "Rocky."

But over all the years, the majority of the crew members have been very good and the guests have been treated to excellent service. The glue that makes it all stick together is Dewey Smith, a good looking "Dude"—why no woman has plucked him off, I'll never know. I guess the proper title for Dewey would be superintendent of Yes Bay. If anything needs to get done, Dewey either does it or sees that it gets done—a remarkable guy.

Sea Emergency

Probably the saddest and most trying experience in my many years in Alaska occurred as follows: my two guests were Germans from Germany. The older (65) could speak English; the younger (55) could not. We were halibut fishing off brow about a 20-minute run from the lodge. The younger guest had hooked a nice halibut. As he was bringing it up as if his life depended on it, he kept repeating "Halibut, halibut!" After successfully landing a 45 pound halibut, the weather was deteriorating, so I started heading for calmer waters in Neets Bay. At this point, the older guest said, "My friend doesn't feel well." I looked at the ailing guest. His face was contorted and he was slobbering. I immediately got on the radio to Yes Bay, but I got no answer. So I got on the radio to the coast guard and said, "Any boat between here and Ketchikan relay a message. I have a guest who appears to have had a stroke. Immediately the coast guard responded, "What is your location? We have a Promech plane in the area." But it turned out the weather conditions were not suited for a landing. The seas were really building. Finally, the Coast Guard advised me to return to Yes Bay. They dispatched a larger medic helicopter to the lodge. When it landed on the dock, it blew everything off the dock. The guest was flown to Ketchikan and put on a medic jet to Seattle, where I understand he made at least a partial recovery.

Big Catch

On a more cheery note, I was guiding two gentlemen during the silver season. The older of the two was an invalid. I headed for the Bushy area near the south end of Neets Bay. The younger guest had landed a couple of silvers. Now it was his partner's turn—bang! His line snapped off the down rigger with a scream of line going out and then the biggest silver I've ever seen made a huge leap—10 feet into the air. I said to the younger one—perhaps you should take it. It is a very big fish. He said "Oh, no. My buddy can handle it." His buddy just stayed in his seat and did a masterful job of fighting the fish. I tried to maneuver the boat to keep him straight off his side of the boat—one final leap, and I thought, "Don't let it throw the hook" as he splashed back into the water. The guest nursed the fish into the net. It weighed just over 20 pounds. That qualifies as a trophy silver. What a fish, what a fisherman!

The Big One that Got Away

I had as my guest a father and a son-in-law. Their sole goal was to catch a large halibut. The first day, we were successful in catching a nice limit of salmon. Our crab and shrimp pots produced favorable quantities of Dungeness crab and shrimp, but no halibut.

The second day, we headed for "Sea Lion Cove," a neat spot about a 20-minute run from the lodge. We dropped down two lines baited with chunks of herring when we arrived. We were in 180 feet of water, not far from shore. Almost an hour passed by and no halibut. We did land a small pacific cod, which we cut the tail off and added to the bait on one of the lines. No sooner had that line hit the bottom and the rod took a terrific bend and line peeled out. "Fish on!" at last. The guest wasn't gaining any ground on the fish, so I tightened up the drag. The procedure is to reel down to the water, then raise the rod up to about chin high and then reel down as you lower the tip to the water. The guest was doing a great job. However, no sooner had he gained several yards, the large fish would regain it. By this time, the guest was perspiring and showing signs of exhaustion.

Almost 20 minutes later, the "biggie" was just below the boat. Seeing the boat, it made another dive. Finally we got it up to the side of the boat—none of us could believe the size of this monster—huge!—a mouth so large you could fit a small kid's head in it. And then, disaster—I took careful aim with the shaft with the detachable spear head (which is attached to a line buoy). With a tremendous thrust, I let it go, aiming just behind the gill plate. At this point, we had two connections to the halibut—a shark hook in its mouth held by a rope with one guest. The line from the rod—hooked in the halibut's mouth by the other.

But talk about "horse-pucky" luck—when the spear hit the halibut, it didn't penetrate deep enough (guide error). The halibut made a tremendous thrust, snapped the fishing line and tore the shark hook out of its mouth and away a winter's supply of halibut went. Talk about three disgusted and frustrated fishermen. An "almost" is almost worse than a "no-fish."

It wasn't until the last hour of their last day of fishing that another chance for a big halibut occurred. We were fishing near the mouth of Yes Bay in 300 feet of water. We'd been fishing in this spot for the better part of an hour with nary a nudge, again using cuts of herring. We were about ready to give up and go in. I said I'll count to 30; if we don't have a hit by then, we'll pull up and go in. 21-22-23-24. Right at 25—bang, a huge hit— how wonderful! How great! Talk about timing. It was the son-in-law again fighting the fish. It must have taken 20 minutes to get it to the surface, but this time, no sudden dives—a little strange? I was all prepared to harpoon it when it reached the surface. At first sighting, it appeared to be a large halibut—same coloring—but on closer view—oh, no! Not a halibut but a large "wing-like skate." We were all so tired and disappointed that we actually began to laugh.

The guest did go home with lots of fish, but no halibut.

To show how fickle fishing can be: a husband and wife fished with me in the same location where the large one was lost and they landed their limit of halibut three days in a row before 9 am each morning. They were guests just prior to the others. I guess that's fishing.

Here's to the Ladies

I had two ladies from Vietnam as guests. They had come to Ketchikan and worked at housekeeping and other tasks. They saved and invested in real estate and had become modestly wealthy.

We had spent the afternoon in Neets Bay fishing for bright chum salmon. We'd almost reached their limits when the ladies said, "Jimmie, we want to catch a halibut." (They called me Jimmie). I said, ladies, we don't have much time but we'll give it a shot. I headed for Yes Bay in a spot off the "crack" in 240 feet of water. (The crack is a cave in the rock wall at the north side of Yes Bay. It's large enough to run one of our boats into it).

We dropped our lines with 16 ounce weight and chunks of herring. In short order, bingo—a nice halibut was on. I had set the hook and handed the rod to one of the ladies and said, "Here's your halibut, ladies, bring it up."

"Oh, no, Jimmie, you bring it up," was their unison response.

I got the halibut to the surface and tried to hold onto the rod and harpoon it at the same time. The harpoon head glanced off the halibut and it dove back down 240 feet. Bringing it again to the surface, I was successful in subduing a nice halibut that was just a shade under 50 pounds. The ladies were ecstatic.

What Brings Them

It's interesting to note what attracts guests to Yes Bay Lodge. I've questioned guests from England, Germany and the USA. Their response is usually, "It's the only lodge where we can fish only one or two persons to a boat." The lodge attends sportsman's shows in various parts of the country to develop business. But probably at least 60 percent come as repeat guests.

Groups like the Paul Gould group, who book the entire lodge each year. The group is involved in investments and the movie industry. Some of the regulars in this group are Paul Gould with his handsome dogs, Sandy Climan and his sons, George Sigler and his sons and George Kolinsky. In the past, the group also included Kirk Douglas and many of his friends.

Another large group is headed by John McAllister, with at least 26 members this year. They ended up taking home three-quarters of a ton of salmon, halibut and rockfish.

Then another regular group are the Mahoneys. As I understand it, they have the contract for maintaining all the trees and greenery for Orange County, California. It's interesting how the Mahoneys started coming to Yes Bay. Peter Gwosdof, an attorney and regular guest at Yes Bay was representing the Mahoneys in a legal matter. During the proceedings, Pete asked the judge for a brief recess to meet privately with his client. In the private room, Pete said to the Mahoneys, "I have only two openings in my group at Yes Bay. How about it?" The Mahoneys said "yes" and they've been coming to Yes Bay ever since.

In addition, guests at Yes Bay include the heads of Bush's Beans, Visa, Bumble Bee Tuna, Atlas Roofing and many more—also lots of salt of the earth folks, dads and moms, sons and daughters.

In addition to the great fishing and food, the lodge is everything you've dreamed a sportsman lodge should be—a large place with a roaring, crackling fire, mounted moose, huge salmon, bear rugs, and halibut carved in beautiful wood. A magnificent view of the bay. Yes, Alaska and Yes Bay has got it all.

Transportation and Communication

The lodge is served by two handsome red, white and black DeHavilland Beaver aircraft. They get you to and from the lodge in less than 30 minutes each way. You can be very confident as you're in the hands of two more than qualified pilots, Mark and David. The lodge is equipped with Wi-Fi and satellite phone.

A fantastic website has been maintained by Capt. Jim Lucas, one of our guides, now in a fill-in position. He is also a great photographer of the outdoors. Catch his works on Facebook.

Alaska More than Fishing

In addition to fishing, there are so many interesting things and beautiful places to view and visit in the Yes Bay area of Alaska. One interesting spot is the Neets Bay Hatchery, located at the very back of Neets Bay.

It's about a 35-minute boat ride from the Yes Bay Lodge. The facility is a co-op between the hatchery, the fishermen, processors and marketers. The hatchery raises and releases young salmon, primarily chum salmon, to the ocean. When the grown salmon return, many are caught by commercial trollers, purse seiners and sport fisherman. The remaining are routed into a processing center where their eggs are removed and sold primarily to companies in the Orient as roe for human consumption. A certain number come into a viewing area where the eggs are removed and male sperm is sprayed over the eggs. Thus fertilized, the eggs are placed on trays in an incubation room. When they reach an acceptable size, they're released into the sea to grow to maturity.

But the real highlight of visiting the hatchery is watching the bears feasting on the salmon in the nearby stream. The bears (mainly black bears) are very selective. They prefer the females and their eggs. They'll jump in the stream and grab a female salmon and bite the middle out, which contains the eggs, and discard the remainder for the seagulls, quite a sight to see.

Another beautiful spot to visit is Shrimp Bay to view the water falls, about a 35-minute boat ride from the lodge. Many guests take advantage of flying to nearby mountain lakes to fish. Another favorite of crew and guests alike is a visit to Baily Bay Hot Springs, again about a 35-minute boat ride from the lodge.

The beauty of the area is breathtaking. Snow-capped mountains reaching up over 3000 feet and azure blue and green melting glacier water at Bell Island. A full moon rising at the entrance of Yes Bay, silver flashing, gleaming on the water, and an occasional late-spawning salmon splashing in the water. This just has to be a true paradise, a God-given blessing. Yes, this is Alaska. This is Yes Bay—come and enjoy!

MOON RISE
YES BAY, ALASKA

Also by the Author

Inspirational Nautical Poems and Prose to Keep You on Your Toes

Positive Poems and Rhymes to Encourage Your Times

Positive Thoughts for a Profitable Day

Making the Principles of Success a Habit

Contact

For comment or additional information, Jim Bernard can be reached at:

JamesBernard711@aol.com

503-680-2366

James Scott Bernard

Author/Publisher

870 N.W. Fir Ave.

Warrenton, OR 97146

Made in the USA
Monee, IL
04 June 2022